Inspiring
Women
Every Day

GW00854519

Plus ... Special Article, Ministry Report and CWR Events Page

MIX
Paper from
responsible sources
FSC® C015900

CLAIRE MUSTERS

Claire is a freelance writer and editor, mum to two young children, pastor's wife, worship leader and school governor. Claire's desire is to help others draw closer to God through her writing, which focuses on marriage, parenting, worship, discipleship, issues facing women today. To find out more about her, please visit www.clairemusters.com or follow @CMusters on Twitter.

FIONA VEITCH SMITH

Fiona Veitch Smith is a writer, editor and university lecturer living in Newcastle upon Tyne. Although born in England, she grew up in South Africa where she became a Christian at age 11. Fiona is now an elder and lay preacher at Heaton Baptist Church. She is the author of a number of books, including the *Poppy Denby Investigates* series and the *Young David* and *Young Joseph* picture books. You can get to know Fiona more at www.fiona.veitchsmith.com

Copyright © CWR 2015. Published by CWR, Waverley Abbey House, Waverley Lane, Farnham, Surrey GU9 8EP, UK. Tel: 01252 784700 Email: mail@cwr.org.uk Registered Charity No. 294387. Registered Limited Company No. 1990308.
Front cover image: Stocksy/ Javier Pardina
Concept development, editing, design and production by CWR. Printed in England by Linney Print.

WEEKEND

Called to God's holiness

For reflection: 1 Peter 1:13–16

'just as he who called you is holy, so be holy in all you do.' (v15)

I t is so exciting to be exploring the subject of holiness together this month. I think it is a theme that can be somewhat overlooked these days, but I believe it is important for us to have a clear understanding of it, as it helps us to lead our lives well.

The starting place for such a study *has* to be God. Too often, when we think of holiness, our minds immediately turn to all the things we think we should be doing and know we aren't. And yet, while that *is* the place our passage starts, it all stems from the fact that God is holiness itself. Yes, He does call us to be holy, and we do need to remember and not belittle that, but He does so because *He* is.

So let's start by looking at the majestic holiness of God, as it is only when we truly understand His holiness that His call for holiness from us makes sense. His holiness far surpasses what human holiness can achieve because, in essence, it is the fact that He is God. What is incredible is that God Himself chose to find ways in which He could commune with His people – and offers us ways in which to partake of holiness for ourselves. This weekend, take some time to thank God for choosing to come close to you and ask Him to reveal more about holiness as you work through these notes.

Optional further reading

Leviticus 19:2; Psalm 29:2; Psalm 96:9

A vision of **our holy God**

Revelation
4:1–11

"'Holy, holy, holy
is the Lord God
Almighty," who
was, and is, and is
to come.' (v8)

**Holy God, the
elders and living
creatures all
responded to
Your holiness
with never-ending
worship. As I
learn more about
Your holiness this
month, may that
be my response
too. Amen.**

Today's verses were given as a vision of heaven's throne room to John. The rich, descriptive language gives us a sense of opulence and majesty. Much has been made of the symbolism: for example, the 24 elders are said to represent all of God's redeemed people (as there were 12 tribes of Israel in the Old Testament and 12 disciples in the New Testament). The four living creatures are symbols of God's character. Before the throne is 'a sea of glass'. Commentators speak of how rare glass was in New Testament times, so this highlights the magnificence of God.

Whatever can be deduced from the symbolism, what is clear is that it is depicting God's awesomeness and holiness. The living creatures are constantly declaring His holiness; the phrase they use repeats the word 'holy' not just twice but three times. The Hebrew word 'holy' (*qadosh*) means 'separate' or 'set apart' and was used to describe the 'otherness' of God. I think the repetition shows us how vital an understanding of His holiness is. When we think of Him, it is not an attribute, such as love, compassion or gentleness – all those that we find safe and familiar – but holiness that should be uppermost in our minds. The elders' words remind us of how His holiness is partnered with glory, honour, power and authority. They recognise that all that is created has only been created because it was His will. His power and authority are different to ours – infinitely greater. The elders are wearing crowns, so have the signs of authority themselves, but lay their crowns before the One that they know has an authority that far surpasses theirs. What a vision!

Acknowledging God's greatness

Exodus 15:1–19

'Who is like you – majestic in holiness, awesome in glory, working wonders?' (v11)

This song was penned by Moses after God miraculously delivered His people from the Egyptians by parting the Red Sea for them and then allowing the water to gush back over those pursuing them. Moses begins by worshipping God for what He has done, describing how He 'hurled' Pharaoh's army into the sea. But he goes on to talk about what it is in God's character that caused Him to act as Israel's salvation. He is saying through this that God's mighty acts reveal His majesty, power and holiness. Look, for example, at verse 7: 'In the greatness of your majesty you threw down those who opposed you.' The language that Moses uses reveals how incredible his God is – that with a simple blast of His nostrils the water was parted. Verse 11 states that there is no one – no god – like God, and later verses talk about how the surrounding nations will hear of what God has done and tremble. Interestingly, Moses also affirms the belief that God will lead His people to His 'holy place' (see v13).

God's holiness can be seen reflected throughout the passage: in His destruction of Pharaoh, His hatred of sin, His wrath against those who refuse to turn from sin and His faithfulness in rescuing His people.

Moses wrote this song for the whole of Israel to sing. It was a way of honouring God for His rescue – a way of giving thanks for His glory. Israel's God-fearing leaders often led the people into offering God a holy, consecrated song or prayer. Even today, homegrown worship songs and prayers can help local congregations to thank God for the specific ways He has revealed His holiness to them.

For prayer and reflection

Thank you Lord that all Your actions reveal Your holiness. Help me to take the time to recall how You rescue and keep me, and then give You praise and thanks for doing so. Amen.

A **right response**

Psalm 96:1–13

'Worship the
LORD in the
splendour of his
holiness; tremble
before him, all the
earth.' (v9)

This psalm may well have been written by David, as it sounds similar to a hymn of praise he wrote in 1 Chronicles. It is a call to the people of Israel to declare the majesty and wonder of God to all the nations surrounding them. It is all about worshipping God because of 'the splendour of his holiness' (v9). As in previous passages, we see various attributes of God listed, such as his glory, splendour and majesty. What is interesting is how the psalmist tells the earth to 'tremble before him' in verse 9. This is another aspect of God's holiness: it should cause us to honour Him with a reverential awe.

God's holiness is absolute – and His wrath, or judgment, comes out of His desire to preserve that holiness in the world. However, this sort of language is not fashionable these days; we don't talk about wrath, judgment and awe very much today, do we? And yet, even back in the 1960s, A.W. Tozer recognised that when we allow human trends and opinion to colour our understanding, then we lose something of our understanding of holiness/God. In his book *The Knowledge of the Holy*, Tozer said: 'The Church has surrendered her once lofty concept of God and has substituted for it one so low, so ignoble, as to be utterly unworthy of thinking, worshipping men ... With our loss of the sense of majesty has come the further loss of religious awe and consciousness of the divine presence.'*

How fully we worship God is based on our knowledge and understanding of Him – in today's reading we are called to reflect on how awesome God is and to 'ascribe' or give Him the kind of worship that He deserves. Spend some time doing this today.

**For prayer
and reflection**

**Lord, forgive
me that I don't
always seek to
understand Your
character more
fully. I see how
it informs my
worship. Help me
to take the time to
learn more about
You. Amen.**

*A.W. Tozer, *The
Knowledge of the Holy*
(HarperCollins, 1961)

CWR MINISTRY EVENTS

DATE	EVENT	PLACE	PRESENTER(S)
May	Great Chapters of the Bible: Great is Your Faithfulness	Waverley Abbey House	Philip Greenslade
May	Transformed by the love of the Father	WAH	Liz Babbs
May	Christ Empowered Living	WAH	Mick and Lynette Brooks
May	Small Groups Rebooted	WAH	Andy Peck
5–20 May	May Country Break	Pilgrim Hall	Pilgrim Hall Team
May	Church Leaders' Forum	WAH	Andy Peck and Pete Greig
9–21; 6–28 May	Counselling Certificate, Module 2	Singapore	Ron Kallmier and Anna Clarkstone
3–26 May	Counselling Certificate, Module 2	Cambodia	Ron Kallmier and Anna Clarkstone
–4 Jun	Partners' Break	PH	CWR Team
–14 Jun	Bible Discovery Weekend: Vital Connections	WAH	Philip Greenslade
0–24 Jun	Introduction to Biblical Care and Counselling	PH	John Munt and Team
2 Jun	Ten things to know about the Old Testament (evening)	WAH	Philip Greenslade
3 Jun	IWED Summer Day: 'Give it A Rest'	WAH	Judy Moore
9 Jun	Ten things to know about the New Testament (evening)	WAH	Philip Greenslade

Please pray for our students and tutors on our ongoing BA Counselling programme at Waverley Abbey House and Pilgrim Hall, as well as our Certificate and Diploma of Christian Counselling and MA in Christian Counselling qualifications.

We would also appreciate prayer for our ongoing ministry in Singapore as well as our many regional events that we are embarking on this year.

For further information and a full list of CWR's courses, phone **+44 (0)1252 784719** or visit the CWR website **www.cwr.org.uk**

You can also download our free daily Prayer Track from **www.cwr.org.uk/free-resources**

'Woe to me!'

'Woe to me! …
For I am a man
of unclean lips …
and my eyes have
seen the King, the
LORD Almighty.'
(v5)

Isaiah describes the vision of God seated on His throne that he was given at the time of his commissioning to be God's prophet. It echoes much of the wording in Revelation 4, which we read a few days ago: the opulence, angels calling out God's holiness again and again. I am always fascinated by the image of God on a throne with the train of His robe filling the whole temple.

What is striking here is Isaiah's response, seen in verse 5. By coming face to face with God's holiness, he instantly recognises his spiritual 'dirtiness'. There is no way he can measure up before such a holy God, so he cries out, 'Woe to me!'. He is about to be commissioned to take God's unpopular word to the people of Israel, and coming face to face with God undoes him. Surely this should be our response, too, as we think on His holiness?

Look at what God does though – He sends a seraph (a type of angel) to Isaiah with a burning coal to touch his lips and tell him that his sins are forgiven. It isn't the coal that cleanses him – only God can do that – but that painful cleansing process was necessary both to encourage Isaiah that he was the right person to be God's messenger, and also to make him ready for his commission. He was being 'set apart' (interestingly, what the word 'holy' means). We too must accept God's cleansing processes in our own lives in order for us to be His messengers to this world.

Isaiah was given this vision of God's holiness in a time when spiritual and moral standards were at an all-time low – sound familiar? We need this type of arresting vision of holiness for ourselves in order not to be dulled to the spiritual decline in our own culture.

For prayer and reflection

I am sorry Lord that so often I just don't see how far our society has travelled from You. Thank You for this reminder that only You can cleanse us from our sin. Amen.

Full of **praise**

1 Samuel 2:1–11

> 'My heart rejoices in the LORD …
> There is no one holy like the LORD
> … there is no Rock like our God.'
> (vv1–2)

Today's prayer of Hannah's is like a song of praise. She talks about how holy God is, but also how He has been her Rock. She celebrates the fact that it is God who is sovereignly in control of what happens, and that He has been in charge since the time He set the world in motion. But just think about the context of this prayer for a moment. Hannah had endured many years of being barren, and being taunted by her husband's other wife who had children. In the temple, as she poured out her sorrow to God, the priest thought she was drunk! But she had continued to be faithful – and so was God.

When she had her son, Samuel, she remembered the promise she had made to God to dedicate him to His service (see 1 Sam. 1:11). She set him apart by dedicating him at the temple and leaving him there with the priest. Imagine that – giving up the one thing you had been desperate for for years. But her prayer, from today's reading, is uttered as she leaves her son there. I find that both incredible and very challenging. Somehow, Hannah understood God's holiness and sovereignty, understood that He orchestrated events throughout history. She had humbled herself before Him and rested in the knowledge that she could trust Him. While she had undergone considerable personal pain over the years, she had seen events with a wider perspective – and God honoured that. Hannah would go on to have more children, and was also able to watch her son grow up 'set apart' to be a prophet in Israel, in the service of kings. Is there something you need to trust God for today?

For prayer and reflection

Heavenly Father, how humbling to be reminded how Hannah, even when she had given up someone so precious, focused on Your holiness and faithfulness. Help me to learn from her example. Amen.

WEEKEND

Our response to God's holiness

For reflection: Psalm 24:1–10

'Who may ascend the mountain of the LORD? Who may stand in his holy place? The one who has clean hands and a pure heart' (vv3–4)

Earlier in the week, we saw how Moses believed that God was leading His people to His holy place. The psalm we are looking at this weekend picks up on many of this week's themes. Again, it is affirmed that God is totally sovereign, but when we consider David's comments about who is allowed into God's holy place, we can be stopped in our tracks, much as Isaiah was. If we are honest, who in this world has clean hands and a pure heart? Who has never lied or allowed a false idol to be a part of their lives?

These verses can be extremely sobering, which is only right, as we need to assess ourselves honestly. This psalm was probably used in corporate worship – I have read that verses 7–10 were used as a re-enactment. The people would call for the temple gates to be opened up, and the priests inside would ask, 'Who is this King of glory?' The group outside would answer, 'The Lord strong and mighty,' etc. Verses 9–10 repeated the process before the temple gates were swung open. All of this symbolised the people's desire to be in God's presence. Do we have this desire, and are we willing to humble ourselves before our holy God this weekend?

Optional further reading
Psalm 86:8–10; Psalm 99:1–3

Becoming a **holy nation**

Exodus 19:1–25

> 'Although the whole earth is mine, you will be for me a kingdom of priests and a holy nation.'
> (vv5–6)

ast week we looked at Moses' song of praise to God for delivering the Israelites. After crossing the Red Sea, they travelled for weeks until they camped at the foot of Mount Sinai. It was on this mountain that God would speak to Moses about why He had rescued them. He had chosen Israel to become 'a holy nation', not because of anything they had done but because He had made a covenant with Abraham (Gen. 15). God wanted a nation that would represent Him on earth, which He could teach His ways to and which, ultimately, would be the nation that our Saviour would be born out of.

We are going to spend this week looking at the various laws, commandments and sacrifices which God instructed Moses that the people needed to adhere to. To us it can seem incredibly confusing and yet we need to understand the reason behind it all.

In Exodus 29:46, God says, 'They will know that I am the LORD their God, who brought them out of Egypt so that I might dwell among them.' Just ponder that phrase for a moment: *So that I might dwell among them.* Isn't it incredible, that the holy God of heaven and earth longed for relationship with His people?

Over the next few days, let's look at the elaborate lengths that God went to in order to bring Israel close to Himself until the appointed time when His Son would be sent. As a perfect, holy being, God cannot entertain sin of any kind: laws and sacrifices were the way in which Israel was able to enjoy God's presence. We can see in today's passage that God instructed Moses to consecrate (make holy/dedicate) the people so that He could appear to them in cloud and fire.

For prayer and reflection

Reflect on the amazing lengths God went to in order to dwell with His people, then spend some time thanking Him that, through Jesus, He has made His home in you.

Commandments to live by

Exodus 20:1–20

'You shall have no other gods before me … Remember the Sabbath day by keeping it holy.' (vv3,8)

In amongst the cloud and fire, God spoke directly to Moses, giving him the Ten Commandments to take back down to the people. So often these are viewed as a list of rules to live by – if we manage to keep them all in our own strength then somehow we will be holy enough to be allowed to call ourselves Christians. However, as Phil Moore points out in his book *Straight to the Heart of Moses*,* the timing of when God gave the commandments is critical. He didn't give them to Moses when he met him at the burning bush and sent him as His messenger to the Israelites in Egypt. They were given *after* God had saved them. They were given to show them how they should respond to the salvation God had provided for them.

Far from a standard that we need to live up to, the Ten Commandments, and indeed the whole Jewish Law, can be seen as a measuring stick of holiness. God uses them to convince Israel – and us – that there is nothing we can do in our own strength to make ourselves spiritually holy.

Interestingly, when Jesus walked the earth He referred back to the Ten Commandments, sometimes even going further than they do (for example, v14 talks about not committing adultery; Jesus in Matt. 5:28 says if a man even looks at a woman lustfully he has committed adultery). No, these commandments were not things for the Israelites – and us – to strive to do. They are to convince us all of the need to accept God's salvation – and holiness. Indeed each commandment says 'You shall' or 'You shall not'. We can read this phrase as a barked order – or a loving promise. Which do you think God meant?

For prayer and reflection

Father, while You lovingly revealed to the Israelites ways in which they could commune with You, I cannot be holy without accepting Your gift of salvation. I do so again today. Amen.

*Phil Moore, Straight to the Heart of Moses (Oxford: Monarch, 2011)

Instructions on **offerings**

'You are to lay your hand on the head of the burnt offering, and it will be accepted on your behalf to make atonement for you.' (v4)

I n the latter part of Exodus, God continues to give instructions to the Israelites on what is necessary if He is to dwell with them. In an amazing act of humility, He tells them that He will come and dwell with them in the Tabernacle which He instructs them to erect in the campsite. One of the Hebrew words used in Exodus to describe the Tabernacle tent is *miqdash*, which means holy place. God also instructs them to set apart priests to work in the Tabernacle. Leviticus starts with God speaking to Moses from the Tabernacle about the types of offerings the people should give. The whole of Leviticus is centred around God's holiness – the very word holiness is mentioned more times than anywhere else in the Bible (152 times).

To our modern eyes, Leviticus seems like a strange, blood-filled book. But just think – God had taken up permanent residence with the Israelites, so they needed to continue to consecrate themselves. If they wanted to continue to enjoy His favour and presence then, as we see in this first chapter, blood *had* to be shed. God said to them in Leviticus 11:44, 'consecrate yourselves and be holy, because I am holy.' In order to approach their holy God, the people's sin had to be atoned for. This first chapter of Leviticus talks about the burnt offering, while the next few chapters cover the other four types of offerings. In each one, it is the perfection of the sacrifice that was so important – and by laying hands on the sacrifice the priest was transferring people's guilt to it. This all points towards the final sacrifice that was to come: Jesus, the Lamb of God.

For prayer and reflection

Loving God, just as blood sacrifice was a way of atoning for the Israelites' sins thank You that Your Son provided a way for us to be saved. Help me never to take that for granted. Amen.

Learning for life

People helping has always been at the heart of our ministry here at CWR. Over the last 30 years, we have pioneered and developed expertise in the area of Christian counselling training. More recently, Waverley Abbey College was established to provide a higher educational arm to CWR, where we continue to develop and run our academic programmes.

Alongside a Christian worldview, the Waverley Integrative Framework is a unique Christian framework, which underpins all of our teaching.

Now firmly established, the College offers both short and long term programmes, from teaching the very foundations of counselling, through to Higher Education Programmes such as our BA (Hons) in Counselling, our MA in Counselling and our MA in Relational Counselling and Psychotherapy programmes, which are currently validated by the University of Roehampton.

All of our tutors are trained counsellors who, along with a dedicated academic support team, work together to continually develop and deliver programmes that maintain academic standards and enhance the quality of student learning wherever possible. By running our programmes as part-time learning, we are also able to offer a flexible way for students to fit studying around their other commitments.

WAVERLEY ABBEY
COLLEGE

Originally, Waverley Abbey House was the location for our training. However, growing student numbers and the popularity of our courses means that Pilgrim Hall now provides the College with the capacity needed to meet the demand for greater availability for accommodation and teaching space.

With over 250 students graduated from Waverley Abbey College, many of whom now work in counselling and pastoral care positions, we look forward to our continued growth and development in helping people learn for life.

For more information on Waverley Abbey College and to order a prospectus, please visit **www.waverleyabbeycollege.ac.uk** or call **01252 784731.**

We have recently welcomed our new Director of Higher Education, Dr Andrew Hartropp to the College. Do pray for Andrew as he leads this area of our ministry forward.

Do not treat **holiness** lightly

Leviticus 9:1–10:3

'Among those who approach me I will be proved holy; in the sight of all the people I will be honoured.' (10:3)

L eviticus 9 sees the priests begin their duties as those who will enter the Tabernacle and sacrifice on the altar on behalf of the people. Moses' brother Aaron and his sons are chosen as priests and the start of our passage details how Aaron follows God's instructions to the letter. We are told that Moses and Aaron then enter the Tent of Meeting and when they come back out God's glory appears. A fire from His presence burns up the offering and the people respond to His presence in joy, but also by humbling themselves, recognising they have just witnessed a display of His holiness.

Unfortunately, there are two among them who don't take His holiness as seriously. Underestimating God, they offer up unauthorised fire to Him – and are consumed as a result. It seems harsh to our modern eyes, but these men had been warned. They had followed God's commands on how to be ordained as priests, which involved a long and complicated process (see chapter 8). They had seen God at Mount Sinai, had heard how God told them not to allow His fire on the altar to go out (in chapter 6) and had seen Moses and Aaron go inside the Tabernacle and emerge unscathed. And yet, at this critical moment, they choose to offer 'unauthorised fire'. It is as if they had grown cocky somehow, or, at the very least, indifferent. Whatever was going on in their minds, they chose to ignore God's command at their peril. The details were there to protect them from God's holy fire; their disobedience cost them their lives. This is a sobering reminder that God is holy; we are not.

For prayer and reflection

Father I can see that You gave strict instructions in order to shield Your people from Your holy fire. I humbly acknowledge You are still a holy God today. Amen

The Day of **Atonement**

Leviticus 16:1–34

> 'because on this day atonement will be made for you, to cleanse you. Then, before the LORD, you will be clean from all your sins.'
> (v30)

For 364 days of the year, the priests were not allowed in the Most Holy Place within the Tabernacle – and yesterday we saw how God's holy fire could simply consume people. During the Day of Atonement, however, the priests were instructed to go in to make atonement for the sins of the nation as a whole. As we can see at the start of this passage, Moses had been warned after the death of Aaron's sons that the priests were not allowed to enter the Most Holy Place whenever they wanted. This means that on the Day of Atonement the priest (here Aaron) had to go through elaborate preparations before he could enter past the final curtain placed in front of the atonement cover on the Ark of the covenant. The Hebrew word *kaphar* means 'to cover over' and was used to describe the lid of the Ark. The word can also be translated as 'atonement'. This Day of Atonement was a day of great celebration, and yet it only *covered over* Israel's sins. Only Jesus' sacrifice would allow for the removal of sins so, until that day, the people needed the priests to cover their sins in this way.

It is interesting to note that there are two goats here – one sacrificed and another sent out into the desert. This is really significant, as it shows God was not only forgiving their sins through the sacrifice, but was removing them from sight, thereby taking away both their guilt and shame. What a great picture of what Jesus does for us! It seems only fitting that God instructed the people to celebrate the Day of Atonement as a day of rest, in order to mark it as special.

For prayer and reflection

God, You not only made a way to cover over Your chosen nation's sins until Your Son's appointed time on earth, but You also dealt with both our guilt and shame. Thank You Lord. Amen.

WEEKEND

Living God's way

For reflection: Leviticus 19:1–18
'"Be holy because I, the LORD your God, am holy."' (v2)

During this week, we have looked at how God set apart the nation of Israel for Himself. He came close to them, dwelling in the Tabernacle in their midst. This, however, necessitated a whole host of elaborate sacrifices and rituals. Verse 2 of our weekend reading really sums up why. His holiness meant they needed to be shielded from the fire that would burn them up, as it did Aaron's sons, if they didn't accept the means by which God was protecting them. This weekend's chapter of Leviticus lists a whole range of laws which, if you look closely, were given as wise counsel. God wanted the best for His people.

We have the same call to holiness today. Fortunately, the times for ritual and obedient outworking of each letter of the law have passed, as Jesus paid the ultimate cost (which we will be looking at in more detail next week). However, we still need to choose to live in the light of the salvation He has bought at such a heavy price for us. Living holy lives should in fact be a heart response to this. Take some time this weekend to reflect on Jesus' sacrifice, and what it means for your relationship with your Heavenly Father.

Optional further reading
Leviticus 23

Jesus **the holy one**

'What do you
want with us,
Jesus of Nazareth?
Have you come to
destroy us? I know
who you are – the
Holy One of God!'
(4:34)

This week, I want us to spend a little time considering how Jesus reflected the holiness of God while He walked this earth. We will be looking at what His sacrifice meant for us in terms of our standing before our holy God later this week.

We know that Jesus was born as a human, and yet the verse in Luke reveals that He was also divine: 'the holy one to be born will be called the Son of God'. This was necessary for our salvation. Just as the animals sacrificed in the Old Testament needed to be without blemish, the One who provided the ultimate sacrifice had to be found to be without sin – to be holy. That is why God had to send His own Son in order to save us.

Jesus showed us how to live, as humans, by the power of the Holy Spirit, and yet through His words and actions, He also revealed who He is. Indeed, the miracles He performed were signs that pointed to His divine nature – and even the demons had to acknowledge who He was, as we can see in today's passage. Before it was ordered out of the man, the demon called Jesus 'the Holy One of God'. While the crowd was amazed at Jesus' power and authority, how sad it was that so few of them recognised who He was. I think that's partly why Jesus asked His own disciples, in Luke 9, who they thought He was. They needed to be clear that He was sent from God in order for them to begin to understand why it was that He was there: not to be the all-conquering, defiant Messiah that would lead them to rise up against their oppressors, but the pure, holy, blameless Lamb that would be slaughtered for their – and our – sin.

**For prayer
and reflection**

**Jesus, it is
humbling to think
about how You
willingly obeyed
Your Father and
came to earth as a
human to enable
us to commune
with Him. Thank
You Holy Lord.
Amen.**

Jesus' **teaching**

Matthew 5:17–30; Mark 9:33–41

'unless your righteousness surpasses that of the Pharisees and the teachers of the law, you will certainly not enter the kingdom of heaven.' (Matt. 5:20)

As I mentioned last week, Jesus' teaching often went further than Old Testament laws. At the start of our Matthew reading, He tells His listeners He's not there to do away with the Law, but to fulfil it. He goes on to use the following phrases a number of times: 'You have heard it said ... But I tell you' (vv21,22,27,28). His standards here seem unreachable but He was calling out the hypocrisy of the Pharisees and teachers of the Law, and also affirming that He is totally holy and without sin. He was providing a fuller understanding of why God had made the Law in the first place; that it was all about the heart. Indeed, He reveals that God already knows what is going on in our hearts when He tells the listeners in our Mark reading that the one who wants to be first should be last. He knew what His disciples were arguing about, so went straight for the heart issue.

What He talks to His disciples about reveals the characteristics of a life of holiness. Not only are we called to be humble and united, but we should love everyone – even those who cannot do anything for themselves, such as little children. In verses 38–41 the disciples are grumbling, jealous of someone who has healed in Jesus' name, more concerned with their group's position than whether any good had been done.

The verses in the rest of Mark 9 reflect what we read in Matthew 5:20–30, where Jesus uses incredibly violent language, not to call us to literal maiming of ourselves but to help us realise how seriously God takes sin – and so must we. Jesus teaches His disciples – and us – how ruthless He wants us to be about living a life of holiness.

For prayer and reflection

Is there anything within Jesus' teaching that you find jarring? If so, explore why you think that is.

Jesus' blood

'he entered the Most Holy Place once for all by his own blood, so obtaining eternal redemption.' (v12)

I t is in Hebrews that we are given the details of how Jesus superseded the Old Testament laws and rituals. When we looked at Leviticus we saw how the sacrifices were a foretaste of what Jesus would do. His sacrifice did far more than they could. While they made people clean or ceremonially acceptable on the outside, Jesus' shedding of blood went far deeper, transforming our hearts to make us clean on the inside. It freed us from sin's power. Of course we still have to walk in that for ourselves, but it did something that we could never do – put us in right standing before God.

Throughout today's chapter, the old is set against the new, revealing the imperfections of the old system. For example, the involuntary sacrifice of animals is set against the voluntary sacrifice of Jesus (see vv13–14).

The verse I have picked out, verse 12, is one that can be a source of great comfort to us. For under the law, people could never be sure of total forgiveness, but Jesus has secured 'eternal redemption' for us. The term redemption is imagery borrowed from slavery. The Greek word *lystrosin* talks about the paying of a price in order to release a slave, which Jesus willingly did for each of us.

Verses 15–17 talk about the legality of Jesus' actions. Using the example of a will, they reveal what Jesus gave us. His love is shown in how He came as a mediator between God and His people – but the benefits could not be experienced until His death. We are unable to meet the demands of our pure and holy God through our own efforts – but Jesus did it for us through His blood.

For prayer and reflection

Jesus, it is fascinating to see how Your sacrifice both reflected and superseded those of the Old Testament. Thank You that You willingly died for me. Amen.

Once and **for all** sacrifice

Hebrews 10:1–14

'For by one sacrifice he has made perfect for ever those who are being made holy.' (v14)

We are continuing to look at how Jesus' sacrifice both mirrored those of the Old Testament and went far further.

Today's chapter starts with a reminder of what a poor, temporary job animal sacrifices did. The first few verses point out that they could never free us from our sin and make us holy – but simply served as a reminder of sin. The old system was, by its very nature, unfinished. The priest had to make sacrifices day after day, and go into the Most Holy Place year after year on the Day of Atonement. But Jesus made a once and for all sacrifice – it does not need to be repeated, as it was perfect.

Today's verses talk about how continual sacrificing was the rhythm of a priest's life, and yet, once Jesus had made His sacrifice, He sat back down next to the Father. He had completely opened the way for God to commune with His people. This does away with any notion that we as humans may be made holy through our own efforts. There is *nothing* we can do. Yes, when we respond fully to the amazing truth of our salvation, we willingly serve and obey God, but that is not the means of our salvation; Jesus has already provided that through His sacrifice.

Interestingly, verse 10 describes us as having 'been made holy', whereas verse 14 talks about us 'being made holy'. This is the difference between justification (I like the explanation 'just as if I'd never sinned') and sanctification (the process of being made holy). When we accept Jesus, God looks at us and sees us as holy, and yet we are on a journey of discipleship – we still need to grow in our holiness.

For prayer and reflection

Think about any times when you have tried to 'earn' your salvation through your own efforts, say sorry to Jesus and thank Him for His once and for all sacrifice.

Taking hold of our **salvation**

**Colossians
1:3–24**

The first part of today's passage reveals how Paul prayed for the Christians in Colossae. It was with an attitude of thankfulness that he prayed. He reminds them of what they have in Jesus – the faith and love that the gospel affords them.

It is interesting to look at what Paul prays in verses 9 and 10: that they may have a greater understanding and wisdom through the Holy Spirit. This is the continuing work of sanctification that God does in our lives. Yes we are reconciled to God through Jesus' death, but we must 'continue in our faith' (as v23 says) in order to live a life worthy of God. That may seem a little like we are being told we need to 'do' in order to please, but the word Paul uses here is *axios*, which means in a manner that is worthy, or in a way that is fitting. This is talking about us living in a way that befits our new identity: holy children of God. How we do this is not through our own efforts but through the Holy Spirit's enabling. It is through His power that we are able to endure, and Paul reminds us that we lay hold of this through an attitude of thanksgiving for how we are now qualified to partake of the inheritance God has called His holy people (v12) to.

Paul goes on to focus on the absolute supremacy of Jesus: that He is the firstborn and holds everything together.

It is only through Jesus that we can be blemish and accusation free – but we need to choose to keep hold of our faith in Him. It is when we recognise that our confidence about our holiness before God can only be found in Jesus that we truly grasp the amazing nature of our salvation.

'he has reconciled you by Christ's physical body through death to present you holy in his sight, without blemish and free from accusation – if you continue in your faith' (vv22–23)

For prayer and reflection

God it is incredible that You view me as without blemish or accusation. By Your Spirit please continue to reveal the fullness of the knowledge of what that means to me. Amen.

WEEKEND

A new identity in Jesus

For reflection: Ephesians 2:1–22

'And God raised us up with Christ and seated us with him in the heavenly realms in Christ Jesus' (v6)

This weekend we see a wonderful picture of how God stepped down and, through His grace, picked us up. The keys to understanding our salvation and new standing before God are His grace and our faith. Verse 8 reminds us that we were saved because of Him but we had to exercise our faith – and still do. We haven't done anything to deserve it, and yet He has created us to do good works. Isn't it incredible to think that, as verse 6 tells us, we have been seated in heavenly places with Christ? This means we now share in His inheritance, as daughters of God. A speaker recently said that he pictures himself being seated next to God, 'having His ear like a child does their parents'. I love that. It reassures us that our prayers *are* being heard.

The second half of today's reading widens out to show how God reconciles both Jew and Gentile in His one family and that those of us who believe are now being built together into a holy temple – isn't that amazing! God's presence is no longer confined to a physical temple but dwells in us. This is also a good reminder that we are part of something much bigger than ourselves.

Optional further reading
Ephesians 1:3–14; Galatians 4:1–7

Choosing to be **living sacrifices**

Romans 12:1–21

'Therefore, I urge you … to offer your bodies as a living sacrifice, holy and pleasing to God' (v1)

T his chapter really hones in on how we should live in response to the gospel. Paul starts with a 'therefore' and also uses the phrase 'in view of God's mercy'. These are the triggers – the response is down to us. While it is true, as we have seen, that we are made holy only through Jesus, and God clothes us in *His* righteousness, we are in the process of being sanctified. And, while that is done through the power of the Holy Spirit, we *do* need to make choices and take action. So many of Paul's instructions here are active: 'offer', 'Do not conform', 'be transformed', 'do not think of yourself', 'Hate what is evil, cling to what is good', etc. James states that faith without works is dead (James 2:14–26) and I think, similarly, Paul is saying here that the process of becoming holy does include us being responsible on a daily basis for choosing to lay down our own agendas and offer ourselves up to God.

I think that often we can shy away from thinking about our own part in our path to holiness. And yet, as Kevin de Young puts it, 'The Bible clearly teaches that holiness is possible. This is good news, not bad news … You are allowed (and expected) to be obedient. You cannot do anything to earn God's love. But as a redeemed, regenerate child of God you don't have to be a spiritual failure.'*

There is also imagery about each one of us being part of a body and that we need to think of the whole and use our gifts to benefit it. As Christians, we need each other. But Paul goes further: our holiness is to impact every area of our lives, including the way we interact with people generally.

For prayer and reflection

Lord, I am humbled as I ponder how the choices I make daily affect my path to holiness. Help me to choose to remember who You are today – and who You have made me to be. Amen.

*Kevin de Young, *The Hole in our Holiness* (Wheaton: Crossway, 2007)

Living the life **already won**

Romans 6:1–23

'now that you have … become slaves of God, the benefit you reap leads to holiness, and the result is eternal life.' (v22)

For prayer and reflection

Lord, I can see that there is no need for me to give in to sin any longer, but that I need to cultivate habits in order to make right choices. Help me to start that today. Amen.

*Jerry Bridges, *The Pursuit of Holiness* (Carol Stream: NavPress Publishing Group, 2003)

**Kevin de Young, *The Hole in our Holiness* (Wheaton: Crossway, 2007)

I n today's reading, Paul starts with a rhetorical question – but answers it quickly with a resounding 'No!' If we continue to sin once we accept the gospel we are belittling both the seriousness of sin and the way that God dealt with it. The language used talks of us once being slaves to sin, but now slaves of God. We can find this language difficult but Paul is using the term 'slave' to underline the fact that we've been bought at a price (see v19 for his explanation). The paradox is that becoming slaves of God is the only way to true freedom.

The problem is, we all continue to sin – why? Often we struggle with sin because we don't fully understand what Jesus did for us. He took us from one kingdom and made us alive in His. We don't *have* to be enslaved to our old sinful nature. The battle can often be in our thinking. Jesus has already killed sin, but we are told in verse 11: 'count yourselves dead to sin'. We need to take hold of this. Sometimes that means practically taking hold of the thoughts in our heads (see Rom. 12:2) that lead to sin and replacing them with biblical truth.

Jerry Bridges, in his book *The Pursuit of Holiness*, explains: 'It is our habit to live for ourselves and not for God. When we become Christians, we do not drop all this overnight. In fact, we will spend the rest of our lives putting off these habits and putting on habits of holiness.'* It takes time and effort to change habits – but the key is in understanding that we are now *in Christ*. As Kevin de Young says, 'The pursuit of holiness is ... the fight to live out the life that has already been made alive in Christ.'**

The testimony of the **Holy Spirit**

Romans 8:1–17

'The Spirit himself testifies with our spirit that we are God's children.' (v16)

Today's passage is so encouraging! We have been looking at the fact that we do need to take responsibility for our sin and yet we are not alone in our journey of holiness. Romans 8 centres around the truth that the Holy Spirit is the one that helps us to experience our salvation and take hold of it fully. Verse 1 begins with a reminder that we are no longer condemned. This is like a breath of fresh air when we are battling habitual sins daily. We don't need to beat ourselves up and promise God we will try harder – we need to remember that the Holy Spirit works inside us to navigate our minds and actions so that they are focused on what pleases God.

Note that Paul says, 'if anyone does not have the Spirit of Christ, they do not belong to Christ' (v9). Turning this on its head, we can view it as a great promise – if we have accepted Jesus as Lord we do have His Spirit living inside us. Our tussles with sin can make us doubt that, but it is important to remind ourselves that He lives inside us and will help us to live holy lives. Interestingly, verses 12 and 13 talk about our obligation to live by the Spirit – but that it is through Him that we do this.

What comes next is such an incredible truth. We are no longer slaves to fear but have been given a Spirit of sonship (or daughtership). We have been adopted and have become God's children. We've already talked about how this makes us heirs with Christ – today's verses show us that it is the Holy Spirit who reminds us of this fact, who testifies to our spirits that we are children of God. What an amazing gift from God!

For prayer and reflection

God, thank You that Your Holy Spirit lives inside me, reminding me that I am Your child, and enabling me to set my mind on those things that please You. I am so grateful. Amen.

A **holy nation**

1 Peter 2:4–10

'you are a chosen people, a royal priesthood, a holy nation, God's special possession' (v9)

Lord, You have called me, and my fellow believers, to be Your holy nation. Help us to live and work in unity, revealing Your glory to those we come into contact with. Amen.

*Warren Wiersbe, Be Hopeful: How to make the best times out of your worst of times (1 Peter) (Colorado Springs: David C Cook, 2009)

This passage is reminiscent of the way that God referred to the Israelites – how He set them apart to be His people. There is further Old Testament language used here: the holy priesthood and spiritual sacrifices. Isaiah 28 is quoted, reminding us that Jesus is the stone that God's holy temple is built on. The amazing thing is that we not only get to be God's holy dwelling place, we are knitted together with others into a much bigger 'spiritual house'.

We saw yesterday how the Holy Spirit testifies that we are children of God. Here we are being reminded that the truth is even bigger than that. We gain a sense of perspective through this reading; it isn't just about you or me as an individual. Yes, we are important and precious to God, but we are part of a 'chosen people', a 'holy nation' that God has set apart for Himself. As we saw with the Old Testament passages we looked at earlier this month, a lot of Scripture focuses on corporate holiness. That is why I wanted to include 1 Peter 2 in our study – to show that it wasn't just an Old Testament concept. It is also a good reminder that we are not to focus on ourselves but live in the light of the fact that we are stones being built into the same building as our fellow believers.

We have seen how in the Old Testament 'God's people *had* a priesthood, but today God's people *are* a priesthood.'* In biblical times especially, it was a privilege to be a priest – today all that we do, individually but also together, should therefore be for God's glory. As verse 9 tells us, the responsibility of our shared calling is to 'declare the praises of him' to the world around us.

Ananias and Sapphira

Acts 5:1–11

'You have not lied just to human beings but to God.'

(v4)

Y ou may be wondering why I have put today's passage in these notes. I feel it follows on well from yesterday's look at corporate holiness. In the previous chapter of Acts we read that the believers shared their possessions and made sure no one was in need. It is a fantastic picture of unity. And yet, even amongst the infant Church, there was a couple who chose to hold back and lie. Their story seems reminiscent of what happened to Aaron's sons and I think it challenges us not to think of God's holiness too lightly now we are post-Old Testament sacrifices.

In his book *Holiness*, John White raises the whole issue of God still being dangerous post-the cross: 'It is quite true that God's love is the most self-giving love. It has redeemed us and has already imparted to us a sanctification and a righteousness that could never be won by law. But we cannot take it for granted. Our souls may be saved, but our physical lives can be endangered if we grow careless about the holiness of divine things.'*

I think that is what was happening here. Ananias and Sapphira were punished not because they chose to hold back some money for themselves – their land and their offering were their own to decide what to do with – but because they lied and took it for granted that it wouldn't matter. They revealed hearts that had a real lack of respect for the truth and being honest with God and His people. Note how the rest of the church responded: 'Great fear seized the whole church' (v11). They had a sudden reminder that God is holy and does not treat sin lightly. I wonder whether today's church could do with a similar reminder ...

For prayer and reflection

Lord, so often we treat Your holiness too lightly. You cannot entertain sin; help us individually and corporately to remember that. Amen.

*John White, *Holiness* (Westbury: Eagle, 1996)

WEEKEND

Hidden in Christ

For reflection: Colossians 3:1–17
'your life is now hidden with Christ in God.' (v3)

This week we have looked at what it means to have new life in Christ, and how we should live as a result. We've seen the importance, both individually and corporately, of truly comprehending our standing in Christ, as it is the key to our holiness. As we've read in many other verses, this passage continues to use the word 'therefore'. Because we are now alive in Christ there are things we need to 'put to death' (or destroy the power of) and virtues we are instructed to 'clothe' ourselves in. The virtue that binds them all together is love. We are given a picture of how the individuals in a church can come together to praise God but also encourage and teach one another.

What I really want us to focus on this weekend is the small phrase 'hidden with Christ in God'. I love this phrase, and it reminds me of when Moses asked to see God's glory. God told him that He would hide him in a cleft in the rock as He passed by because Moses couldn't look on God's face and live due to His holiness. Similarly, we are now hidden in the rock of Jesus, safe and secure.

Optional further reading
Exodus 33:12–23; Ephesians 4:1–16

Running with **perseverance**

Hebrews 12:1–14

> 'let us throw off everything that hinders and the sin that so easily entangles.' (v1)

During the last two days of May, let's remind ourselves of some central truths that we have discovered during this month. Today's reading is a great motivational passage to help us run our race of life well, refusing to give in to sin. It teaches us to remember Jesus and how He lived His life with His goal always before Him. There is a 'big picture' being painted here, which is there to help strengthen us in those moments when we feel like giving up our efforts.

We are also told to 'Endure hardship as discipline' (v7), as we are God's children, and that 'God disciplines us for our good, in order that we may share in his holiness' (v10). Jerry Bridges in *The Pursuit of Holiness* says that, 'Holiness is ... required for our well-being'* and makes the point that God's discipline is a way in which He enables us to become holy. He disciplines us because He loves us and desires to have the type of close relationship a father has to his child.

Again, we see the word 'Therefore' being used in verse 12. There is a sense that we need to be responsible and disciplined in our lifestyles and that it isn't just for our benefit. We are to be good examples to others and live at peace with one another. I have ended today's reading with the reminder that 'without holiness no one will see the Lord.' Yes, holiness is a gift freely given, but if we long to see God we must run hard after it. I love how Kevin de Young puts it: 'To run hard after holiness is another way of running hard after God'.** It isn't holiness as an end in itself that we are seeking, but the One in whom it is all hidden: Jesus.

For prayer and reflection

Father, help me to understand the unending love that is behind Your discipline, and that seeking holiness is really seeking to know Jesus more. Amen.

*Jerry Bridges, *The Pursuit of Holiness* (Milton Keynes: Authentic, 2004)

**Kevin de Young, *The Hole in our Holiness* (Wheaton: Crossway, 2007)

A **prayer** for holiness

1 Thessalonians
3:12–13;
2 Timothy
2:21–22

'May he
strengthen your
hearts so that you
will be blameless
and holy in the
presence of our
God and Father'
(1 Thess. 3:12)

Today's verse, which I have chosen from 1 Thessalonians 3:12, is my prayer for you as we end this study on holiness together. The verses in today's reading talk about how it is Jesus who makes us strong and enables us to love one another. Not only that, Paul is reminding the Thessalonian church that it is the Holy Spirit alone who can strengthen them – from the heart outwards. He does this for each one of us, in order for us to be 'blameless and holy' before God.

During this month we have looked at how holy our God is, why blood sacrifice was necessary for us to have a restored relationship with Him, and the responsibility we have to pursue holiness. In our final day together I want to come full circle, back to a reminder that, for all the efforts that we *do* need to put in, becoming holy is based on our standing in Christ and the work that the Holy Spirit does within us.

As we have seen, holiness means being set apart. Two Timothy reminds us that vessels can be used for both noble or common uses. Paul was urging Timothy to allow God to use him for His higher purposes. I love the way *The Message* translates verse 21: 'Become the kind of container God can use to present any and every kind of gift to his guests for their blessing.' There needs to be a willingness to set aside our own agendas and bow to God's will for our lives in order to be made holy and to bless others. But that is also the way to satisfaction and fruitfulness. Remember: we have been made alive in Christ – becoming holy simply means becoming more the people that we were created to be.

**For prayer
and reflection**

**Lord, thank You
that in You I am
blameless before
God. I recognise
that continuing to
pursue holiness is
the way to become
the person You
want me to be.
Help me to do so.
Amen.**

In 2015, over 1,300 churches, groups and individuals took part in our first National Prayer Weekend. Gathering prayer requests from their neighbours, thousands of people spent a fruitful weekend in September praying for God to work in their communities.

As well as from our local Christian community, we had some amazing and unexpected prayer requests from as far as Australia, South Africa, Romania, Spain, Cornwall and the House of Commons, as well as prayer requests from a number of folk who would never usually admit to having a church connection!

Following on from the encouraging feedback of last year, we want to enable and encourage individuals, groups and churches to continue to reach out to their communities through prayer, changing people's lives by encountering God. Therefore the date has now been set for another National Prayer Weekend to be held on the **23–25 September 2016**.

If you have any feedback from your 2015 National Prayer Weekend, or would like to join in and find out more about the **National Prayer Weekend 2016**, please visit **www.national-prayer-weekend.com**

Fruit that will last

Known by **their fruit**

'By their fruit you will recognise them. Do people pick grapes from thorn-bushes, or figs from thistles?' (v16)

I once had a chilli plant growing in my kitchen. Year after year it produced the hottest little chillies you could imagine. And it was beautiful too. I loved my chilli plant and actually shed a tear when it died after my house sitter forgot to water it when I was away on holiday. Fortunately, I had dried some of the chillies so I used them to replant. I prepared the soil with the best compost I could find, planted the seeds, watered them and put them on a sunny windowsill.

About a month later the chillies began to grow. But one plant outdid its siblings: the shoots were greener, the leaves bigger and the first flower was enormous. It was only when the fruit began to form and became round and bulbous that I realised that it wasn't a chilli, but a bell pepper. I now have a scrawny chilli plant in the same pot as this high achiever, but because their root balls are so entwined I can't separate them.

In today's passage, Jesus is warning people about the fruit of false prophets. They appeared to be one thing but turned out to be something else. However, this principle can be applied more broadly to all people and all Christians. We will be judged, not by our potential or what we claim to be, but what, in the end, we finally produce. By their fruit you will know them.

We know that only good trees produce good fruit, but we also know that by ourselves we cannot be good. In the month ahead, may we co-operate with God in the production of good fruit and may it be fruit that will last.

For prayer and reflection

Lord, we ask that You, the Great Gardener, will help us prepare our soil for the seeds You want to plant in us. We know that only good trees produce good fruit. Amen.

Fruit that will **last**

'Every plant that my heavenly Father has not planted will be pulled up by the roots.' (v13)

The bell pepper I told you about yesterday turned out to be a bit of a one-hit-wonder. It bore one gorgeous, tasty, fleshy red fruit, but that was it. Meanwhile, the little chilli took its time and finally produced a small, but significant crop. I had to decide between keeping the flashy pepper or the faithful chilli, as the former was slowly strangling the latter. One needed to be cut back so the other could grow.

After more than 30 years of being a Christian, I've come to realise that real fruit takes a long time to grow. In fact, it will take a lifetime. Now there's nothing wrong with new Christians showing fruit early on, but the really good stuff often takes longer to mature. The fruit of the Spirit is God-grown. These are the things that reveal our true selves as God moulds us into the people He wants us to be. Often they grow out of difficulties, conflicts and trials.

Jesus is talking about pulling up a plant that should never have been planted in the first place. This may apply to our lives – something that should not have even been planted, but was. However, there's a different kind of pruning that Jesus refers to in John 15:2 – the cutting back of some of the early, enthusiastic growth so something better can emerge.

How ever long we've been a Christian we need to ask: am I loving, joyful, peaceful and kind? Am I gentle, patient, faithful and self-controlled? Are these what emerge in a stressful situation, when people and circumstances put me under pressure? If not, then God's got a bit more work to do with me. This garden is still a work in progress.

For prayer and reflection

Lord, so often we disappoint You and ourselves but we know that we can trust You to prune us and tend to us in Your quest to produce fruit that will last. Amen.

A new **direction**

Isaiah 30:19–33

'Whether you turn to the right or to the left, your ears will hear a voice behind you, saying, "This is the way; walk in it."' (v21)

I have a very enthusiastic rose that grows under my kitchen window. It has fragrant orange blooms that it can't wait to show off. It grows so quickly that I have to cut it back at least twice in the growing season, as well as giving it a good prune in late autumn. If I don't, it quickly covers my kitchen window, cutting out the light.

At first I thought I had been blessed with an abundant supply of roses to cut and bring into the house. But I was disappointed – within a few hours the roses wilted. I realised that the flowers were simply to be enjoyed where they grew. But the kitchen window was a problem.

Some years ago a child swung on my garden gate and broke it, and I had never got round to replacing it. Then one day I had the idea of installing a trellis arch over the open gateway and training my high-performing rose to grow over it instead of the window. I pruned the upward growth but left the lateral shoots and tied them to the trellis – after one season they had covered half the arch! However, I still have to keep a close eye on it as, given half a chance, it claws its way back to the window. Hopefully it will eventually get the message and grow where I want it to – where it does not obstruct the light and will perform a useful function for the rest of the garden.

It's the same in our spiritual lives. We sometimes put all of our energy into the wrong things and need to be trained to go the way God wants us to go. But, like in today's passage from Isaiah, we can trust that God will always guide us towards the best way.

For prayer and reflection

Are there areas in your life that are constantly being blocked? Do you feel you are being channelled in a new direction? Could this be the Lord at work in you?

WEEKEND

Thirsting for God

For reflection: Psalm 42

'My soul thirsts for God, for the living God. When can I go and meet with God?' (v2)

A Dry White Season

It's been a dry white season
of sun and heat and
the smell of sunscreen on
browning shoulders.
It's been a dry white season
of dried-up puddles
like cracked, brown watercolour
shuddering to dust.
It's been a dry white season
of wilting leaves and
shrivelling roots and hard
unsweetened fruit.
We need the rain.

Optional further reading
John 15–16

Introvert or extrovert?

'the fruit of the
Spirit is love,
joy, peace,
forbearance,
kindness,
goodness,
faithfulness,
gentleness and self-
control.' (vv22–23)

A s someone who is socially confident and creative, I used to believe that a good Christian should be the opposite of me. Surely quieter, more reserved people are naturally more gentle, faithful, patient and self-controlled? For many years I believed my extrovert personality was a curse that kept me from being a better Christian. Wasn't 'performance' showing off? Didn't it lead to pride?

But after some misguided attempts to deny that part of me – including refusing to 'perform' in public – I accepted that to do so was to deny who God had created me to be. I realised that if anyone else thought I was showing off, it was their issue not mine.

The fruit of the Spirit is not personality-dependent, because that wouldn't be fair. God created some of us with vivid colours and others with pastels and He loves us all.

Whether we are introverted or extroverted all of us can be loving, joyful, peaceful, patient, kind, good, faithful, gentle and self-controlled. We don't have to produce these things by simple hard work or as a by-product of our natural personalities. They are evidence of God's presence in us.

So what is the fruit? In verse 22, it is referred to in the singular although there are multiple aspects of it (love, joy, peace, etc). This is because the Holy Spirit is an individual and the fruit comes from one source. It also means that unlike the gifts of the Spirit (eg 1 Corinthians 12) we should manifest *all* of the fruit – although different aspects may develop at different rates. Over the next few weeks we will look at each of these in more detail.

**For prayer
and reflection**

**Father God, thank
You that You have
created each of
us to be different,
and yet You
require all of us
to manifest Your
fruit to the world.
Amen.**

Loving others as you love yourself

'Love your neighbour as yourself.' (v39)

Love is our natural birthright as a Christian – it's internal evidence of the Spirit within us. The *doing* aspect of love – the fruit of the Spirit – is the external evidence for the world to see. We have love in us because God *is* Love; it's getting it out that's the problem!

Jesus tells us that the greatest commandment is to love God with all our heart, mind and strength, and the second is to love others like we love ourselves. There's one big obstacle to that kind of love: our*selves*. To love like this means we have to put aside our own needs, wants and comforts for the sake of others. With a natural instinct for self-preservation, that's a hard thing to do.

This selfless kind of love costs. If you want to know how much, look at what Jesus did: He considered our needs above His own – and it killed Him! That's pretty potent love.

Notice though that the first command is to love God. That's because we cannot hope to love others unless we love God first and allow His love to flow through us. Love is a choice not a feeling, but you may find that the more you choose to put others first, the more you actually feel like doing it.

Start small: leave the biggest slice of cake for someone else. Then work your way up to giving away things that really hurt. For me it's time. If I'm resentful of it, I know that I'm not really acting out of God's love in me.

As we discovered yesterday, each of us is different and the Lord will have different ways to develop love in you. Ask Him to show you ways to put love into action and consider other people's needs before your own.

For prayer and reflection

Dear God, help me to love as You love. Help me not to be content with mere feelings of love but to act upon them. Amen.

When love's **not deserved**

'love your enemies and pray for those who persecute you' (v44)

We spoke yesterday of sacrificial love: loving others before ourselves, even – and especially – when it costs us. But what happens when we think people don't deserve that kind of love? The thankless teenager, the unrepentant criminal, the faithless spouse? What does love like that look like? For me, it's the willingness to extend forgiveness and restore relationship before it is even asked for or desired by the opposite party. That's how God loved us when we were far away from Him and that's what His love through us will do when someone has wronged us.

How can we love our enemies? Many years ago when I was a new and impressionable intern, I was hurt and exploited by a woman in authority over me. In addition to the way she treated me, I also discovered some horrible truths about her personal life. Since then she has gone on to be extremely successful in her field, winning national awards and being lauded as a kind of cultural saint.

All this time I have been working on forgiving her; and I thought I had done. But each time I read about her in the paper I think: she doesn't deserve that! This was despite me knowing that she is very good at her job and most definitely – on a professional level – deserves all the plaudits she has received.

Then God spoke to me and said: 'The day you can be genuinely happy for this woman's success, will be the day you have truly forgiven her. That is love.'

Who are you holding grudges against? What unforgiveness lies in your heart? If you are given an opportunity to help someone who doesn't deserve it, what will you do?

For prayer and reflection

Father, You tell us to love and forgive our enemies. Thank You that as the fruit of Your love grows inside us we can draw on it to do what seems impossible. Amen.

When love gets **manipulative**

'My son ... you are always with me, and everything I have is yours. But we had to celebrate and be glad' (vv31–32)

Today we meet a father whose love for his son never diminished, even when it was rebuffed. But we also read of a brother whose sacrificial acts were a counterfeit form of love.

If you apply the definition of love as putting others' needs before your own, then the older brother in this story appeared to be very loving. He was the good son, the one who stood by his dad, helping on the farm and doing his duty while his brother went off gallivanting.

But what was his motivation? One gets the feeling that he was doing it to earn his father's love in the hope of inheriting the whole estate. His brother had been paid out in cash, so, by default, the property would become his. This brother was making sure his investment was well looked after. Of course, that may not have been his conscious plan; he may have thought he was supporting his dad and being a good son because it was the right thing to do – the loving thing. It was only when his wayward brother came back and his position was threatened that his true motivation came to light, perhaps even to himself.

Sometimes I need to examine my motives for loving – or appearing to love – others. What am I hoping to get out of it? We can see this ugly form of salvation by works rearing its head when we start keeping lists of the good things we've done for people. 'After all I've done for them,' we say. This is not God's way of loving. He loves people whether or not they love Him in return. That's unconditional love. That's God's love.

For prayer and reflection

Dear Lord, help me to examine my motives for loving others. Please shine Your Spirit of Truth on those dark areas of my heart. Amen.

Surprised by joy

Zephaniah
3:14–17

'Sing, Daughter
Zion; shout aloud,
Israel! Be glad and
rejoice with all
your heart' (v14)

C.S. Lewis called his autobiography *Surprised by Joy** – the story of how he turned from a cynical agnostic to be one of the greatest Christian writers of the twentieth Century. But why was it such a surprise?

Because, to some, God has a bad reputation. He is seen as strict, dull and judgmental by many people in the world. In his book *Simply Good News*, Tom Wright refers to the popular perception of God as 'the old bully in the sky'.** Who is to blame for this image? Well, if we are supposed to be a reflection of God to the world then perhaps it is us; those of us who call ourselves Christians.

Yet joy is a fruit of the Spirit. If the Spirit of God is living in us it should be our *normal* state of being. Joy is not the same as happiness. Happiness is based on *happenings*, frequently out of our control. But joy comes from a much deeper well.

Joy is the natural response to freedom: a dog let off its leash, a child on a bouncy castle, a bird freed from its cage – this is joy unbounded. How much more should our natural response be when we are set free? Joy is not just something to look forward to as our heavenly reward; it can and should be enjoyed now.

The Bible is full of feasts and festivals and celebrations and we are invited to join the party. Our God, the host, is a happy God, a joyful God, a God full of laughter with an awesome sense of humour. And we, created in His image, cannot help but be the same. En*joy*!

For prayer and reflection

Dear Lord, thank You that You are a God abounding in joy and laughter. Help me to release that joy as I revel in the freedom I have in You. Amen.

*C.S Lewis, *Surprised by Joy* (London: Bles, 1955)

**Tom Wright, *Simply Good News* (London: SPCK, 2015)

WEEKEND

A spiritual MOT: Part 1

For reflection: Philippians 2:1–18

'continue to work out your salvation with fear and trembling, for it is God who works in you to will and to act' (vv12–13)

I f you own a motor vehicle you will know that once a year you have to take it for a roadworthiness test or an MOT as it's known in Britain. This is to show that your vehicle is safe to travel on the road and passes a test of roadworthiness.

Today, we are going to do a brief spiritual MOT to see where we are on the scale of fruitfulness. This is obviously not a definitive examination, just a bit of fun, but it might give you an insight into your spiritual health. Looking at the spiritual qualities below, rate yourself on a scale of 1–10, with one being barely more than a pip and 10 being the best of the best on the allotment:

Loving

Joyful

Peaceful

Patient

Kind

Good

Faithful

Gentle

Self-controlled

Optional further reading

Barbara Johnson, *Stick a Geranium in Your Hat and Be Happy* (Nashville: Thomas Nelson, 2010)

Sorrow and **joy**

Psalm 30

'You turned my wailing into dancing; you removed my sackcloth and clothed me with joy' (v11)

Joy is God's calling card. Sometimes this is a special grace, a divine visitation to empower us for a particularly difficult task or to comfort us during a trial. Many of the great saints and martyrs, such as Dietrich Bonhoeffer who died in a Nazi concentration camp, testify to being overcome by waves of joy in the midst of suffering. The psalmist echoes this in Psalm 94:19: 'When anxiety was great within me, your consolation brought joy to my soul.'

Joy and sorrow can, and do, frequently co-exist. Sorrow is so frequently a partner of joy because it is only when we experience the former that we look deep within ourselves and are surprised by the latter. This is not optimistic, fake, happy-clappy religiosity, but an accurate depiction of what the Christian life can and should be.

I have suffered from depression. I have had my fair share of health problems, financial difficulties and bereavements. I am not in denial of reality. Christians, like everyone, are not immune to suffering, sadness and depression.

However, although these negative feelings may be there for a season, I believe they should not be the norm. Joy should be allowed to return and do its work. It's a wonderful gift that can bring healing to us, and the people around us.

We need to recognise that although sorrow might visit for a night, joy will follow in the morning. Even though it's hard to believe sometimes and we feel that we're just hanging onto faith by our fingernails, the God of joy is always faithful.

For prayer and reflection

Dear Lord, I pray that during the hard times You will help me to dip into the well of joy within. Amen.

The joy of the **Lord**

**Psalm 126;
Proverbs 17:22**

'A cheerful heart
is good medicine,
but a crushed spirit
dries up the bones.'
(Prov. 17:22)

You may have heard it said that 'laughter is the best medicine'. Well, that's a quote from the Bible. Godly wisdom tells us that a positive disposition, undergirded by the spiritual fruit of joy, brings health to our bodies, minds and spirits.

In more modern times, there have been scientific tests and trials showing the benefits of an optimistic disposition and the healing qualities of humour. Research done by Dr Michael Miller at the University of Maryland Medical Center suggests laughter is similar to exercise in that it decreases blood pressure, increases muscle flexion, improves overall performance of the heart's muscular functions and possibly wards off heart disease. Some hospitals even provide 'laughter therapy' for cancer patients.

It also has a positive impact on reducing emotional and psychological disorders such as depression and anxiety. A review in the online psychiatric journal *Current Psychiatry* found that 'depression reduces the frequency of laughter and, inversely, laughter reduces the severity of depression'. Laughter, they reported, also increases the connectivity of patients with people in their life, which further alleviates symptoms of depression.

Of course there's a difference between human wit and godly joy. Comedians are often some of the most depressed people in show business and the tragic clown is a familiar figure. But I truly believe that allowing God's joy to flow out of us and manifest itself in a healthy sense of humour will do wonders for our lives as well as the Church's reputation in the world.

**For prayer
and reflection**

**Thank God for
laughter and
the wonderful,
healing gift of joy.
Commit today to
look on the bright
side of life this
week.**

Introducing Paraclesis: Journeying Together

The *Daily Guide* is part of
CWR's new six-week Paraclesis:
Journeying Together church
initiative, designed to help
you come alongside others
to care. This practical,
engaging workbook guides you
through what Scripture says
about journeying and caring,
encouraging you to interact with
the gift of your journey and the
people around you.

'He brings us alongside someone else
who is going through hard times so that
we can be there for that person just as
God was there for us.'
(2 Cor. 1:3—4, *The Message*)

Fellow Travellers

Caring is a commitment, an action
of the will that embraces the truth
that 'It is more blessed to give than
to receive' (Acts 20:35). It is more
than just a feeling whilst you are
in a moment, or a good mood, or
an emotional response. To be a
fellow traveller with someone on the
journey of life is a commitment of
time and resources. The idea of such
a commitment can strike fear into
our hearts. We can worry we will not
have what it takes, have enough time,
resources and experience, and like the
disciples at the feeding of the 5,000,
we may feel inadequate for the task.
'I am not a counsellor, psychotherapist,
experienced social worker or pastor,'
we say, 'that hurting person needs
expert help I cannot give.'

Recently when I was diagnosed
with kidney cancer, my world was
thrown into confusion. Although
my family and I knew the same God

was with us after the diagnosis as before and He had not changed, our circumstances had. They brought with them a new set of unfamiliar challenges as I faced major surgery to remove the malignant tumour and diseased kidney. In these difficult days of adjustment, we did not need a professional counsellor, psychotherapist or a cognitive behavioural therapist to help us in our struggle, but fellow travellers who had been this way before, who could journey with us in our hour of need. I called someone I knew who had trodden that pathway before us, who became a fellow traveller and companion on our recovery journey, and like Jesus with the Emmaus Road disciples, they brought hope, commitment and consolation to our lives.

But they also brought something else; I describe this as their 'gift of journey', their personal life experience and journey with cancer, grace and truth. Through this person, we received strength, encouragement, healing and insight as we were sustained through a difficult passage in our journey. How sad that often in the church, this huge resource (people's experience on their own journeys) is largely neglected, wasted or untapped. These journey experiences should be spiritual resources, made available to us through Jesus Christ in the family of God. Such a wealth of life experience is deposited in the lives of God's people – people who in their lives have experienced deep issues of the soul and life circumstances. Paul writes, 'I feel certain that you, my brothers, have real Christian character and experience, and that you are capable of keeping each other on the right road' (Rom. 15:14, Phillips). Are you one of these people? Then make a commitment today to let God use your gift of journey to come alongside others.

Extract taken from week 3, day 4 of the *Daily Guide* by Trevor J. Partridge. ISBN 978-1-78259-417-8.

Sign up now to learn more about Paraclesis, purchase resources and receive a starter pack so you and your church can begin your care journey together. Visit our website **www.paraclesis.org.uk** for more information.

Peace with God

'Therefore, since we have been justified through faith, we have peace with God through our Lord Jesus Christ.' (vv1–2).

Self-help movements are geared towards one thing: finding and keeping inner peace. What these movements miss is that the prerequisite for peace with ourselves is peace with God. There is only one way to true peace: a saving relationship with Jesus Christ.

What does it mean to be at peace with God? Peace is the absence of enmity or discord. Nothing stands between us: no grudges, no guilt and no unfinished business. The result of that peace is an easy relationship where we are comfortable in God's presence.

This wonderful state of being, this fruit of the Spirit in our lives, is a result of our reconciliation to God through Jesus' death and resurrection. When we ask Jesus to come into our lives and free us from everything that stands between us and God (aka 'sin') the slate is wiped clean and we can finally be at peace with God.

Unfortunately, the slate doesn't stay clean. As human beings we are prone to sin and put at risk the peace we have with God.

For prayer and reflection

You may have drifted from that place of peace with God – or perhaps you've never found it? Ask Jesus now to come into your life and bring His peace.

How far can we push Him? There is a theological debate about whether or not we can lose our status of 'being saved' if we continue to sin without repenting (see for example Heb. 10:26–29 which warns us not to push God too far). Many books have been written about that and many prayers spent agonising over it. I don't know the answer, but what I do know is: if we confess our sins, God will wipe the slate clean again and again (see 1 John 1:9). A lifestyle that seeks to be at peace with God is one that reflects true salvation. Once you've tasted peace, do not let it go.

Peace with **others**

'Blessed are the peacemakers for they shall be called children of God.' (v9)

Yesterday we spoke about finding peace with God being the only way to find inner peace. But it shouldn't stop there. Once we have peace with God and peace with ourselves, we need to bring peace to others. 'Blessed are the peacemakers', said Jesus in that wonderful teaching we know as the Sermon on the Mount – a blueprint for godly Christian living.

Peace on earth is one of God's goals. This peace will only be fully established when the Lord's Kingdom-rule is extended throughout the world at His second coming, when evil will once and for all be extinguished. Until then, there will be pockets of peace, as the angel proclaimed, in 'those on whom his favour rests' (Luke 2:14). It is the job of every Christian to extend the peace that is ours to influence the world around us.

This job can take many forms. One way is to refuse to engage in any activity that spreads strife. Refraining from sharing a juicy piece of gossip, choosing not to respond in kind when your irritated spouse snaps at you, biting your tongue and not having the last word in an argument and backing down from 'road rage', are all ways in which the enemy of peace – enmity – can be stripped of its power.

Another way is to be a mediator or bridge-builder. The willingness to see both sides of an argument is something that should be cultivated. However, I'm disappointed to say that I rarely see it enough in Christians, myself included. The aggressive, uncompromising stance of much of the Church has done a lot of damage. Yes, we are called to be defenders of the truth, but let's be careful that we don't do more harm than good in the way we do it.

Father, I pray that the Spirit of Peace will flow through me. Show me how to be a bridge-builder and a peacemaker. Amen.

Give me **patience**

2 Peter 3:8–18

'But do not forget this one thing, dear friends: with the Lord a day is like a thousand years, and a thousand years are like a day.' (v8)

Inevitably, when I complete a spiritual MOT like we did last weekend, patience is the thing that scores lowest. I can be a very impatient person. In my line of work as a freelance writer and lecturer, deadlines are very important and I have little tolerance for people who frequently flout them. I also like to be on time and am impatient with my daughter when she drags her heels in the morning and we have to run like Usain Bolt to get to school.

In addition, I like to see results quickly and don't have much patience for my students who haven't learned what they need to at a certain point in the academic year. This is my natural instinct and it's something I continually try to work on.

I thank God that He is more patient with me than I am with others. God teaches me a lot about patience through my garden. I have been working on my current garden for 12 years and it is finally becoming what I hoped it would be when I first moved in and planted those seedlings and shrubs.

Compost is another thing. When I first started making my own compost, I expected to be able to use it within one year. I have discovered that it takes about three years to make good compost and that what I put in the top of the bin needs to fester and rot for a lot longer than I first thought.

Being in my garden slows me down and helps me see that the best things take time to develop. I cannot and should not expect immediate results. A seed planted today will not grow overnight, and in some cases might not grow at all. I need to allow others the same grace. I need to allow it in myself too. Give me patience, Lord – but in Your time.

For prayer and reflection

In what areas of your life do you need to develop patience? Ask the Lord to help you be more patient today.

Fruit that blesses

For reflection: Psalm 1
*'That person is like a tree planted by streams of water,
which yields its fruit in season' (v3)*

The Old Apple Tree
It has stood in the field, in the corner,
For generations of swings and lovers
And things and travellers
Who rest their backs on its bark.
It has spread out its limbs, for seasons,
Of perches of birds and root
Holes of hedgehogs and caterpillars
Who crawl on the dapple of leaves.
And it has given its fruit, so freely,
To hands and to pockets and to
Picnic baskets and bakers of pies
Who serve it hot with cream.
But if it were to speak, or whisper, perhaps,
Of purpose and growth and
Trying to be,
It would shrug its old trunk and simply say:
'What's all the fuss? That's me.'

Optional further reading
Revelation 21–22

Long-suffering

Colossians 1:3–14

'We also pray that you will be strengthened with all his glorious power so you will have all the endurance and patience you need. May you be filled with joy' (v11, NLT)

I n the NIV 2011 translation, the fourth fruit of the Spirit is 'forbearance' (Galatians 5:22) – to put up with or to not be disturbed very easily. Other translations use the word 'patience' and still others 'long-suffering' – or, as in the NLT scripture, endurance. In my own personal life, my father has taught me what long-suffering means.

When I was 15, my mother had back surgery that went wrong. No one is sure what really happened because the medical profession closed ranks and no one would give us a straight answer. But the overall result was that my mother had brain damage and developed severe grand mal temporal lobe epilepsy.

She was unable to continue with her job as a manager of a shoe shop. She could never be left on her own. Trips to the shops would often end with seizures in the aisles and some people saying to my face that she was demon possessed (this was in South Africa).

Another time she was chopping vegetables, had a seizure and lunged at me with a knife repeatedly before she collapsed. I knew she didn't mean it, but my then 16-year-old self was traumatised.

At 19, I was able to leave and go to university. I visited home regularly, but the day-to-day care was left to my dad who did it – without complaint – for the next 28 years. My mother died of unrelated lung cancer three years ago. I arrived two minutes after she died. My dad had been with her all night.

While I was growing up, my father was never a patient man. Like me, small things would irritate him; but when it came to the big things in life, the important things, he was long-suffering. I marvel at the beauty of it.

For prayer and reflection

Think today of someone you know who is long-suffering. Now, hold them up in prayer.

Common **courtesy**

Luke 17:11–19

'Jesus asked: "Were not all ten cleansed? Where are the other nine?"' (v17)

The *Collins English Dictionary* defines kindness as the quality of being: 'considerate, friendly and helpful. Having a warm-hearted nature; pleasant or agreeable.'

Certain societies or cultures encourage courtesy, good manners and 'agreeableness' more than others. However, being polite and well-behaved on the outside does not necessarily mean you are kind on the inside. I watched the film *The Last King of Scotland* (2006) the other day and was struck by how pleasant and urbane Idi Amin appeared. In many cases, kindness is only skin-deep.

That being said, I bemoan the decline of courtesy. One of my pet hates is opening the door for someone and standing there like a doorstop while people walk through ignoring me; or stepping out of the way in a supermarket to let someone's trolley through while they walk straight past me without a glance.

Common courtesy is not the fullness of kindness, but it's a start. It boils down to considering others' needs before your own, or at least not being so self-absorbed with your own life that you don't notice other people and their needs. Sometimes a simple 'thank you' can make someone's day. I can let through a line of traffic whose drivers drive past as if I didn't exist, but then the one person who waves and smiles restores my faith in human nature.

I wonder if that was what Jesus was thinking when the one leper came back to say thank you. The other nine had received the greatest gift they could possibly imagine and yet forgot a simple act of courtesy.

For prayer and reflection

Make a point today to notice other people and to be kind and courteous when you can.

Global kindness

2 Samuel 12:1–13

'You are the man!' (v7)

Kindness is outward-looking, naturally considering others before yourself. Selfishness is inward-looking, considering yourself first.

David was made aware of his selfishness when Nathan told him a story of a rich man with vast flocks who took a poor man's only sheep. David was so caught up in pursuing his own needs and desires (remember the context of this passage is David's pursuit of Bathsheba, a married woman) that he did not stop to consider the reality of what it might be like to live in someone else's shoes. David had many wives; Uriah, Bathsheba's husband, had only her. Leaving aside the obvious sin of adultery – and murder! – the other lesson of this story is about how people who have much often forget there are people who have little.

I believe we need to apply this principle on a global scale.

Consider Fair Trade. We need to remember what it costs – in human terms – to enjoy our coffee, chocolate or bananas; and the sweatshop conditions of children who make the cheap clothes we buy. Being prepared to pay a little bit more for goods is actually an act of kindness. It is taking the trouble to consider how our actions affect others and a small way of putting our 'self' in its place.

Then there's the issue of being kind to the earth. By limiting our consumption of the world's resources, we are being kind to future generations. Now, while Christians should guard against allowing environmentalism to be our path to salvation, I believe that good stewardship of resources and promoting just trade practices should be a natural reflection of our faith.

For prayer and reflection

Reflect now on what you regularly buy. Is there a way you can choose a Fair Trade option instead – even if it costs a little more?

July

WRITTEN FROM THE HEART
CATHY MADAVAN

August

JOURNEY OF FAITH
MARGARET HUGHES

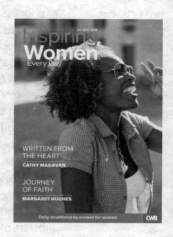

In **July**, Cathy Madavan turns to the book of Philippians and explores Paul's letter, line by line. With her usual warmth, Cathy highlights that in encouraging his friends, and us, to live a life for Christ, Paul's writing covers a deep sense of commitment to the Lord, whatever happens.

In **August**, Margaret Hughes looks at how walking with God is a journey of faith, and shows us how many events in the Bible happen as part of a journey during which people encounter and learn of God. Margaret's explorations take us on a journey of discovery, leading us to grow in our faith and knowledge of God, and His amazing love for each one of us.

Obtain your copy from CWR, Christian bookshops or your National Distributor. If you would like to take out a subscription, see the order form at the back of these notes.

Also available as eBook/eSubscription

A force for **good**

Acts 2:42–47

'They sold property and possessions to give to anyone who had need.' (v45)

Goodness is often confused with kindness. It is also misunderstood as a synonym for righteousness, becoming simply the opposite of badness, sinfulness or naughtiness. However, the word translated to 'goodness' in the New Testament comes from the Greek word *agathosune* which literally means 'beneficence'. This old English word means charity or generous giving. It is the root of the word benefactor – one who gives for the benefit of others.

Giving out of goodness can be of our time, energy, money, gifts or talents. We see a need and we meet it in the best way we can, motivated either by mercy or a sense of doing what is right. This is different to kindness, which is motivated more from consideration and courtesy. Kindness manifests in individual, sometimes random acts. Goodness is manifest in a *lifestyle* of giving.

Goodness causes us to contribute positively to the community. Someone acting out of goodness might give up their time to work with a homeless charity, whereas someone acting out of kindness might give their sandwich to a homeless person on the street.

William J. Booth, the founder of the Salvation Army, certainly performed many kind acts in his daily life, but it was his goodness (or rather God's goodness in him) that caused him to set up an organisation dedicated to alleviating physical and spiritual poverty.

Goodness actively stands against the forces of evil in the world: poverty, suffering (mentally and physically) and spiritual slavery or injustice. One hears of people or organisations being a 'force for good'. When Christians corporately act against evil the Church becomes this force.

For prayer and reflection

Father God, You are a good God. May Your goodness work through me today as I seek to meet other people's needs. Amen.

Faithful Barnabas

Acts 15:22–35

'our dear friends
Barnabas and Paul
– men who have
risked their lives
for the name of our
Lord Jesus Christ.'
(vv25–26)

A gain, in writing these notes, I turn to the fruit of my garden. The other day I was making a lamb stew and wanted to add some basil. I have some growing in my herb garden. So I popped out with a pair of scissors only to discover that in the two days since I'd last looked at it, the basil had shrivelled and died. Now, this is not the first time basil has let me down. Whether I grow it inside or out, it's always prone to being a bit of a drama queen. Disappointed, but not surprised, I decided to substitute rosemary, thinking: 'It's never let me down yet.' And true to form, there it was, solid and healthy and only too happy to help me with my stew.

The *Collins English Dictionary* defines faithful as: 'loyal, consistent and reliable'. Now I know in a Christian context it also means 'having faith', but today I want to focus on the more prosaic meaning.

We all enjoy working with people we can depend upon. It makes communal life, whether in the family or at work, so much easier. How comforting it is to know that someone will put out the bins in time for the collection or deliver that report on deadline. We don't have to stress because we know others will do what they say they will do. That is faithfulness.

St Paul had a faithful companion named Barnabas. Barnabas is mentioned 33 times in the New Testament and – apart from once when they disagreed about a young man named John Mark – he seemed to always have been by Paul's side. Barnabas was the one you could depend upon to never give up, to always be there, to do the job he had committed to do. Are you a Basil or a Barnabas?

For prayer and reflection

Consider your own level of faithfulness. How dependable are you? Commit today to following through on what you've said you will do and be careful not to over-commit in the future.

WEEKEND

A spiritual MOT: Part 2

For reflection: 1 Corinthians 3:1–23

'So neither the one who plants nor the one who waters is anything, but only God, who makes things grow.' (v7)

Two weeks ago, we did a quick spiritual MOT test. Today I would like you to go back to that and look at how you've been getting on. In the last fourteen days, have you been working on any particular area? Have you been challenged or tested in anything? Have you been pleasantly surprised by your response to trigger situations? Have you been on the lookout for ways to help your fruit grow? Here is the list of fruitful qualities again. Now, instead of marking each from one to 10, just write down any thoughts or insights you may have gained in each area over this month.

Loving

Joyful

Peaceful

Patient

Kind

Good

Faithful

Gentle

Self-controlled

Optional further reading

Kieran Beville, *Cultivating Christian Character: The Fruit of the Spirit* (Leominster: Day One Publications, 2005)

New every morning

Lamentations 3:22–33

'his compassions never fail. They are new every morning; great is your faithfulness.'
(vv22–23)

I love my garden in the morning – and so do the birds. We have a flock of regular visitors; some nest in our whitebeam tree or various hedges and shrubs. There are Jenny and Gerald the woodpigeons, Doris and Derek the turtledoves, Daisy and Scruffy the blackbirds, Bertha and Barney the blue tits and Rob the robin. Rob is a roving bachelor but is occasionally joined by a lady-friend that my daughter and I have named Rebecca. We also have regular gangs of sparrows and starlings plus a couple of magpies, George and Mildred, who hang around looking thuggish but never come to eat from the bird table.

I try to keep the table well stocked with seed (to my husband's dismay as he wonders – out loud – how they all possibly survived without me and the local supermarket's fare). But sometimes I forget; other times I'm away from home. I doubt during get-togethers over a pile of worms the birds say to each other: 'You know what I like about this place, the owner never, ever fails to supply our needs – it's new every morning! She's faithfulness personified. Aren't we blessed?'

Fortunately for us, God is a much better caretaker, gardener and father. He *is* faithfulness personified. So how is that manifested in us as a fruit of the Spirit? When we let the truth of God's faithfulness sink into our souls it gives us a sense of security in knowing that God can and always will be someone we can trust. We can put our faith in His faithfulness – and the more we do that, the more it will show in our lives.

For prayer and reflection

Consider an area of your life where you need to have more faith in God's faithfulness. Ask Him now to produce that fruit in you.

Gentleness

Titus 3:1–10

'slander no one … be peaceable and considerate, and always … be gentle towards everyone.' (v2)

As I mentioned yesterday, we have a pair of turtledoves called Doris and Derek. It's no wonder that these birds are often associated with love. They coo to each other and sit on the fence gently nuzzling each other's necks. They seem completely at peace and never seem to get into fights with other birds. On the other hand, we have a pair of magpies, and when they're not stealing other birds' eggs they are squabbling and bickering between themselves. I look at one couple and see gentleness, and another and see strife.

I know people like that. Some people just make you feel relaxed and safe. They are people whose very presence seems to bring healing. This is gentleness – the ability to soothe and minister acceptance and grace. It's one of the most beautiful fruits of the Spirit.

Older versions of the Bible used to translate this word as meekness – as in 'gentle Jesus meek and mild' – but this has connotations of a gentle person being a spineless doormat. Jesus was gentle and strong at the same time. And His Spirit in us produces the same thing.

Gentleness should not mean you are a pushover or that you can't assert yourself when you need to. It just means you don't assert yourself when you don't have to. Gentleness allows other people to be who they really are without judging them. Gentleness refuses to retaliate when someone else is picking a fight. Not because you are weak, but because you are strong in your relationship with God and don't have anything to prove.

For prayer and reflection

Father, please produce in me the fruit of gentleness. Let me not judge or speak to others harshly. Forgive me Lord where I have failed. Amen.

Self-control

Romans 7:14–25

I write this as I reach for yet another chocolate biscuit – even though I'm supposed to be on a diet. Why is it, I ask, that I have so little self-control? Isn't it meant to be a fruit of the Spirit? If I find faithfulness, goodness and joy bubbling out of me, why can't it be the same with self-control?

There are two things to remember: firstly, the fruit do not all develop at an equal rate. The Lord works on some things for a season and leaves other parts for a time better suited to His purpose. The second thing is that self-control is not so much about striving and trying to be better – this goes against all we know about resting in God and allowing Him to do His work through us – but it is more about making a choice to submit ourselves to the control of God.

Self-control is God-control and that is related to surrender – the conscious laying down of what we want to take up what we know God wants. But how do we do that? Well I'm encouraged that even the great saints like Paul struggled with this. Paul recognises that it is sin at work in him, just as it is sin at work in us.

The good news is, we are a work in progress. Although I struggle with some things today, I can look back and see the progress I have made in other areas and know that in His time the Lord will help me through this too. And if I get to the end of my life and still can't resist a chocolate biscuit (or worse!), then I rest in the knowledge that God will love me – and you – anyway.

> 'I do not understand what I do. For what I want to do I do not do, but what I hate I do.' (v15)

For prayer and reflection

Lord, today I give you my lack of self-control. I am so ashamed that I have given in, once again. Lord, I ask for Your forgiveness and Your grace to start again. Amen.

The vine and the **gardener**

'I am the true vine, and my father is the gardener.' (v1)

The danger of reading a month's worth of notes about producing the fruit of the Spirit – including spiritual MOTs every second week – is that it becomes a month of striving and guilt. That is the last thing I want. In living the Christian life, we need to strike a balance between committing ourselves to being transformed into the people God created us to be, and simply resting in the knowledge that God loves us just the way we are anyway. However, He loves us too much to leave us there.

In today's passage, we see the words that Jesus spoke to His disciples the night before He died. Here He gives us some guidance on how we might balance striving for transformation and resting in God. His Father – our Father – is the gardener. He is the one who has created the world and planted us in it. But if we were to be left to our own devices it would be chaos. Have you ever seen a garden that has been left without a caretaker? Nettles take over, the grass grows where it shouldn't and brambles choke the life out of everything they wrap around.

When we ask God to take control of our lives – and remember it is a choice – the garden is taken in hand by the Master Gardener. But there is still work for us to do. We are to grow; we are to bear fruit. However, we can only do it by being connected to the vine who is Jesus. The vine is the centrepiece of God's garden and the lifeblood of our spiritual existence.

If you are struggling to be loving, joyful, peaceful, patient, kind, good, faithful, gentle or self-controlled, focus on Him. Without Him you can do nothing. Remain in Him, daily, allowing the Gardener to prune what needs to be pruned and you *will* bear much fruit. Fruit that will last.

For prayer and reflection

Lord Jesus, today I choose to remain in You. Help me to rest in Your love and allow our Father to do the work that needs to be done so that I can bear fruit. Amen.

ORDER FORM

5 EASY WAYS TO ORDER:

1. Phone in your credit card order: **01252 784700** (Mon–Fri, 9.30am – 5pm)
2. Visit our online store at **www.cwr.org.uk/store**
3. Send this form together with your payment to:
   CWR, Waverley Abbey House, Waverley Lane, Farnham, Surrey GU9 8EP
4. Visit a Christian bookshop
5. For Australia and New Zealand visit KI Entertainment at **www.cwr4u.net.au**

For a list of our National Distributors, who supply countries outside the UK, visit www.cwr.org.uk/distributors

YOUR DETAILS (REQUIRED FOR ORDERS AND DONATIONS)

Full Name:	**CWR ID No.** (if known):
Home Address:	
	Postcode:
Telephone No. (for queries):	**Email:**

PUBLICATIONS

TITLE	QTY	PRICE	TOTAL
		Total publications	

All CWR adult Bible-reading notes are also available in eBook and email subscription format.
Visit www.cwr.org.uk for further information.

UK p&p: up to 24.99 = **2.99**; 25.00 and over = **FREE**

Elsewhere p&p: up to 10 = **4.95**; 10.01 - 50 = **6.95**; 50.01 - 99.99 = **10**; 100 and over = **30**

Please allow 14 days for delivery | **Total publications and p&p A** |

SUBSCRIPTIONS* (NON DIRECT DEBIT)

	QTY	PRICE (INCLUDING P&P)			TOTAL
		UK	Europe	Elsewhere	
Every Day with Jesus (1yr, 6 issues)		15.95	19.95	Please contact nearest National Distributor or CWR direct	
Large Print *Every Day with Jesus* (1yr, 6 issues)		15.95	19.95		
Inspiring Women Every Day (1yr, 6 issues)		15.95	19.95		
Life Every Day (Jeff Lucas) (1yr, 6 issues)		15.95	19.95		
Mettle: 14-18s (1yr, 3 issues)		14.50	16.60		
YP's: 11-15s (1yr, 6 issues)		15.95	19.95		
Topz: 7-11s (1yr, 6 issues)		15.95	19.95		
Cover to Cover Every Day (1yr, 6 issues)		Email subscription only, to order visit online store.			
Total Subscriptions (Subscription prices already include postage and packing)				**B**	

Please circle which bimonthly issue you would like your subscription to commence from:

JAN/FEB MAR/APR MAY/JUN JUL/AUG SEP/OCT NOV/DEC

* Only use this section for subscriptions paid for by credit/debit card or
cheque. For Direct Debit subscriptions see overleaf.

CONTINUED OVERLEAF >>

PAYMENT DETAILS

☐ I enclose a cheque/PO made payable to CWR for the amount of: _____

☐ Please charge my credit/debit card.

Cardholder's Name (in BLOCK CAPITALS) _____

Card No. ☐☐☐☐ ☐☐☐☐ ☐☐☐☐ ☐☐☐☐

Expires End ☐☐ ☐☐   Security Code ☐☐☐

GIFT TO CWR ☐ Please send me an acknowledgement of my gift   **C** ☐

GIFT AID (YOUR HOME ADDRESS REQUIRED, SEE OVERLEAF)

giftaid it I am a UK taxpayer and want CWR to reclaim the tax on all my donations for the four years prior to this year **and on** all donations I make from the date of this Gift Aid declaration until further notice.*

Taxpayer's Full Name (in BLOCK CAPITALS) _____

Signature _____   **Date** _____

*I understand I must pay an amount of Income/Capital Gains Tax at least equal to the tax the charity reclaims in the tax year.

GRAND TOTAL (Total of A, B, & C) ☐

SUBSCRIPTIONS BY DIRECT DEBIT (UK BANK ACCOUNT HOLDERS ONLY)

Subscriptions cost 15.95 (except *Mettle*: 14.50) for one year for delivery within the UK. Please tick relevant boxes and fill in the form belo

☐ *Every Day with Jesus* (1yr, 6 issues)
☐ Large Print *Every Day with Jesus* (1yr, 6 issues)
☐ *Inspiring Women Every Day* (1yr, 6 issues)
☐ *Life Every Day* (Jeff Lucas) (1yr, 6 issues)

☐ *Mettle*: 14-18s (1yr, 3 issues)
☐ *YP's*: 11-15s (1yr, 6 issues)
☐ *Topz*: 7-11s (1yr, 6 issues)

Issue to commence fro
☐ Jan/Feb ☐ Jul/Aug
☐ Mar/Apr ☐ Sep/Oct
☐ May/Jun ☐ Nov/Dec

CWR

Instruction to your Bank or
Building Society to pay by Direct Debit

DIRECT Debit

Please fill in the form and send to: CWR, Waverley Abbey House, Waverley Lane, Farnham, Surrey GU9 8EP

Name and full postal address of your Bank or Building Society

To: The Manager _____ Bank/Building Society

Address _____
_____
_____
_____ Postcode _____

Name(s) of Account Holder(s)
_____

Branch Sort Code
☐☐ ☐☐ ☐☐

Bank/Building Society Account Number
☐☐☐☐☐☐☐☐

Originator's Identification Number

4	2	0	4	8	7

Reference
☐☐☐☐☐☐☐☐☐☐☐☐☐☐☐☐☐☐

Instruction to your Bank or Building Society
Please pay CWR Direct Debits from the account detailed in this Instruction subject to the safeguards assured by the Direct Debit Guarantee.
I understand that this Instruction may remain with CWR and, if so, details will passed electronically to my Bank/Building Society.

Signature(s)
_____
_____

Date
_____

Banks and Building Societies may not accept Direct Debit Instructions for some types of account